NATIONAL GEOGRAPHIC

A WHALING COMMUNITY
of the 1840s

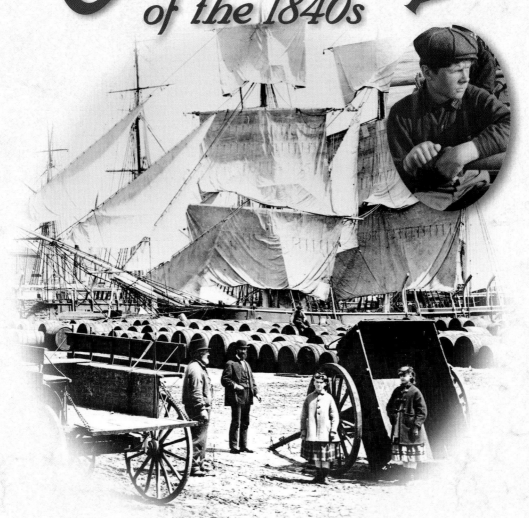

GARE THOMPSON

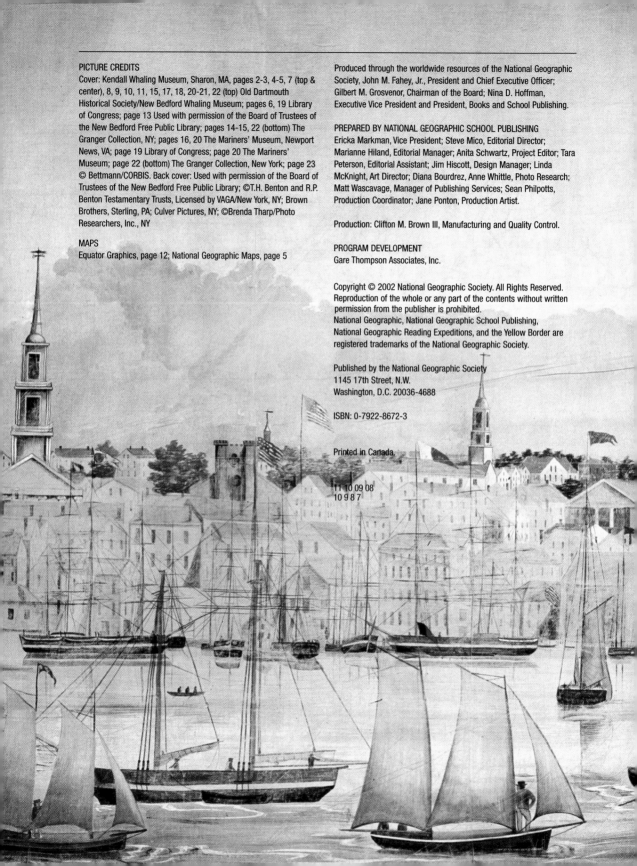

Produced through the worldwide resources of the National Geographic Society, John M. Fahey, Jr., President and Chief Executive Officer; Gilbert M. Grosvenor, Chairman of the Board; Nina D. Hoffman, Executive Vice President and President, Books and School Publishing.

PREPARED BY NATIONAL GEOGRAPHIC SCHOOL PUBLISHING
Ericka Markman, Vice President; Steve Mico, Editorial Director; Marianne Hiland, Editorial Manager; Anita Schwartz, Project Editor; Tara Peterson, Editorial Assistant; Jim Hiscott, Design Manager; Linda McKnight, Art Director; Diana Bourdrez, Anne Whittle, Photo Research; Matt Wascavage, Manager of Publishing Services; Sean Philpotts, Production Coordinator; Jane Ponton, Production Artist.

Production: Clifton M. Brown III, Manufacturing and Quality Control.

PROGRAM DEVELOPMENT
Gare Thompson Associates, Inc.

Published by the National Geographic Society
1145 17th Street, N.W.
Washington, D.C. 20036-4688

ISBN: 0-7922-8672-3

Printed in Canada.

11 10 09 08
10 9 8 7

TABLE *of* CONTENTS

CHAPTER 1

NEW BEDFORD
MASSACHUSETTS
1848

Standing at the top of Johnny Cake Hill, I can see far out into the Atlantic Ocean. The waves in New Bedford **harbor** are gently rocking the many whaling ships waiting at the **docks**. From up here all the people working on the docks look like bees in a hive. They are getting ships ready to go to sea or unloading ships that have just come into **port**. We in New Bedford live for whaling.

My granddad says that the whales we capture in the ocean are our gold. Without whaling, New Bedford would be just another small town on the **coast** of Massachusetts. But instead, New Bedford is the biggest and best whaling community in the United States.

I want to go to sea. I want to be a cabin boy on a whaling ship. But I am only 12 years old, and I have to get my parents to say I can go. Then I will be off to sea. What an adventure! All the Shea men have gone to sea. I, Michael Shea, want to join them.

My granddad says the people in New Bedford have been whaling since the 1700s. The early whalers worked hard. Some of them got rich. They built mansions on Johnny Cake Hill that their families still live in. My dad says the closer to the top of the hill you live, the richer you are. We live close to the bottom. Maybe some day we can move to the top if I make a success of whaling.

My whole family works in the whaling business. In fact, almost everyone I know, except for Widow Parkins, works in the whaling business. Her husband was a captain, but he died at sea. Every day she walks for hours along the widow's walk atop her house, watching the sea. I guess she hopes he'll come back. His body was never found.

Women stand on a balcony, called a "widow's walk," watching for a ship to bring home their husband, father, or brother. ▼

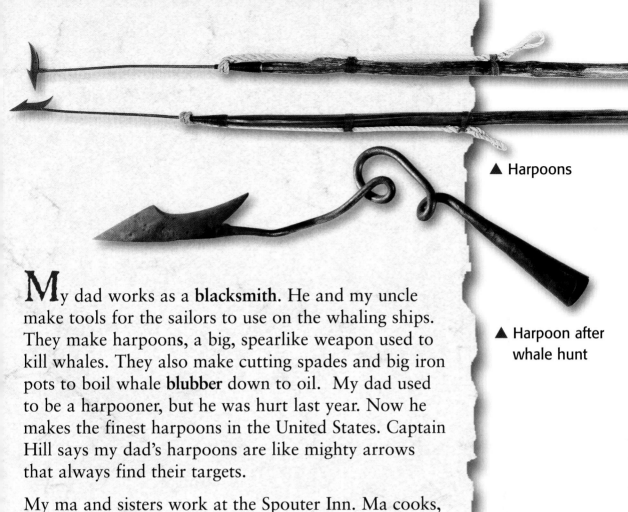

▲ Harpoons

▲ Harpoon after
whale hunt

My dad works as a **blacksmith**. He and my uncle make tools for the sailors to use on the whaling ships. They make harpoons, a big, spearlike weapon used to kill whales. They also make cutting spades and big iron pots to boil whale **blubber** down to oil. My dad used to be a harpooner, but he was hurt last year. Now he makes the finest harpoons in the United States. Captain Hill says my dad's harpoons are like mighty arrows that always find their targets.

My ma and sisters work at the Spouter Inn. Ma cooks, and my sisters serve the meals and clean the rooms. I help, too. Sailors from all around the world stay there.

My granddad says that the sailors used to be farm boys from Maine or New York. Now they're from Africa, Portugal, or the Islands. Some speak different languages and have tattoos. Ma cooks lots of meat stews and serves fresh fruit. Sailors don't get much fresh food on board ship. She is a good cook.

My brothers work at the warehouse. They load and unload barrels of oil and goods such as tea, sandalwood, and food supplies. It's hard work.

7

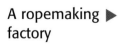

▲ Scrimshaw

Even Granddad still works. He works at the candle shop, Candleworks. They make candles from spermaceti, a fine oil from the sperm whale. Lots of times, though, Granddad and his friends sit on the porch of the store and carve whalebone. Their carvings are called **scrimshaw**. They're beautiful. Stores in big cities like Boston and Newport sell their carvings.

My friend, Tommy Smith, runs errands for one of the agents who signs up sailors for the long voyages. My neighbor, Billy Mackin, works in the rope factory making rope for the ships. Grandma used to mend sails until her eyesight got bad. But I want to go to sea. I want to chase whales like my granddad did. He says it's in my blood. I'll be homesick for New Bedford though. I'll miss the hustle and bustle around the docks. I'll miss my family, too.

A ropemaking ▶
factory

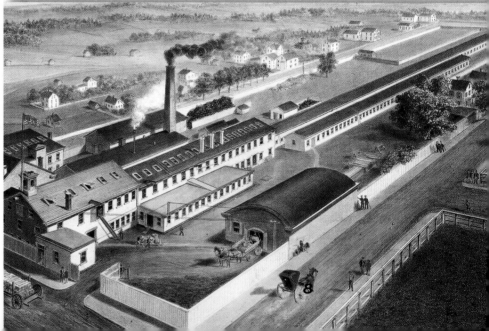

8

CHAPTER 2

LIVING
on a
WHALER

Last night a miracle happened. Captain Hill visited us and talked to my parents. I am to be his cabin boy! Captain Hill promised to watch over me, so Ma and Dad said yes. Wait till Tommy sees me. He was sure my parents wouldn't let me go. Working on the whaler, I'll serve meals and clean the ship.

My dad tells me that I am to do whatever Captain Hill says. He is the boss. Everyone on the ship must obey him. I will work for the cook, too. I can't wait to start.

This morning Dad and I went to the agent's office to sign the **contract,** or agreement paper. Dad let me read the contract before he signed it. My hands shook a little when I read that I could be gone for as long as two years. That's a long time. If we have a successful trip, I will receive a small sum of money. Dad says that success means filling over 2,000 barrels with whale oil.

Dad signed the contract. I am now a cabin boy!

A Crew Wanted,
FOR THE
SCHOONER
SWAN.
Now lying at Fair-
haven, and bound
On a SOUTHERN & BAHAMA
WHALE CRUISE.
Good shares will be given.—— Apply to
JOHN ALDEN.
Fairhaven (N. B.) May 25, 1796.

▲ A poster advertising for a whaling crew

I pack my things in my granddad's old chest. It is the same chest Dad and my brothers used. Ma says it brought them back safely.

I pack light clothes for the hot weather and a warm jacket for cold nights. Ma gives me a sewing kit. I will have to mend my own shirts. My brothers and sisters give me pens and a pad for drawing. I tell them I'll draw many whales.

My granddad gives me a carving knife. Ma has knitted me a soft, warm blanket.

Dad gives me my own **compass!** Real sailors use it to find north, south, east, and west. Dad says that reading a compass is called "boxing it." I will try to make Dad and Granddad proud.

From the deck of the ship, I wave goodbye to my family on the dock. A breeze fills the sails. We're off. The search for whales has begun. The captain calls a meeting. All 32 members of the crew stand quietly on the deck.

In a loud, clear voice he tells us the rules of his ship. We are to obey his orders. His word is law. Each of us has a job to do. We are to do it quickly and well. During a storm, ships can go down in minutes. If we do not follow orders, we will be punished. I will obey him. I do not want to be whipped or get only bread and water to eat for days.

After his talk, the captain goes to his cabin to study his maps. I help him unpack. His cabin is the largest and best room on the ship. It is larger than any two of our rooms at home. He has a big bed bolted to the floor. At the other end of the room is a couch. Opposite the couch is a beautiful wooden desk.

I unpack the captain's books and clothes. Then he tells me to go help Cook in the galley. (It's the ship's kitchen.) On the way, the ship hits rough water. My stomach flip-flops like the ship. I hope I will not be sick.

I serve the meals. The captain and the officers eat first. They eat roast duck, bread and butter, and vegetables. For dessert they have plum pudding and coffee. Then I serve the blacksmith, the cook, and the harpooners. Later, I set out food on the deck for the rest of the crew. They get salt pork, beans, and hard bread. I eat last.

Captain Hill charts our course. Our first stop will be the West Indies. The three officers assign jobs. They divide the crew into watches. Each watch has four men who must work for eight hours at a time. The men look for whales and watch for storms. One crew member climbs the **mast** to look for whales. He is the lookout.

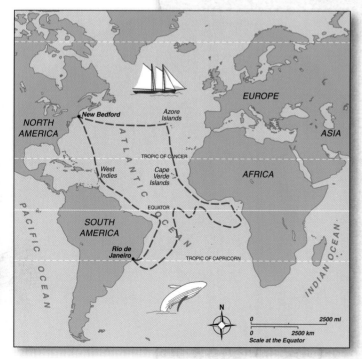

Other sailors polish brass, clean the deck, and prepare the whaleboats. I help cook and clean. Pedro, a sailor from Portugal, and I make friends. The day goes by quickly.

I sleep in the same area as the cook. I am lucky. The sailors sleep in a very small space. It is dark and cramped. My bed is hard, but my blanket is soft and warm. I have to get up at dawn tomorrow. The work will start all over again.

CHAPTER 3

HUNTING WHALES

We have been at sea for five weeks. Each day starts the same. Dawn breaks. Cook screams for me. I help Cook with breakfast. Then I go on deck to clean.

The officers get the whaleboat crews ready. Each whaleboat has an officer who leads them, a harpooner, and a crew of four. For three hours, the crew practices. The captain shouts, "To the boats!" The men fly to the boats and lower them. They quickly row out to sea. Waves hit the boats hard. The men return wet and tired.

Two hours later, the lookout yells, "There she blows!" A sperm whale has been spotted. The captain orders the crews to the whaleboats. Using his **spyglass**, Captain Hill locates the whale. I see her. She is huge.

The boats race toward her. Then they stop. Whales have good hearing, and noise scares them off. We all wait. Will the whale stay on the surface or dive?

The whale dives. The waves rock the whaleboats. I think that the boats are going to sink, but they don't. I hear the officers commanding the men to stay calm. Suddenly the whale looms up right beside one of the boats.

The men are quiet. One wrong move and they will be lost. The men in the other boats begin rowing hard to pull closer to the whale. The harpooner in the first boat raises his harpoon. He gets ready to throw. The officer commands, "Strike!" The harpoon sails into the whale. It is a hit. We cheer. But the hunt is not over.

The whale dives. The line attached to the harpoon flies out of the boat. The whale surfaces. Pulling the boat behind it, the whale races away. Pedro tells me the crew is on a "Nantucket sleigh ride." They fly across the water.

Tiring, the whale slows down. The boatsman's spear hits the whale in the lungs. It is now dying. Our first whale has been captured. Now the hard work begins.

The tired crew tows the 50-ton whale to the ship. We have to cut up the whale quickly. Otherwise, the sharks will get it. The captain tells us that we will work in six-hour shifts day and night until the job is done. The crew ties the whale to the side of the ship with heavy chains.

Cutting platforms are set up. First, the blubber, the thick layer of fat, is cut off. The men use 15-foot long poles to cut it. Cutting blubber is like peeling an orange. The blubber is cut into long pieces, or blankets. They are very heavy.

The blankets are hauled on deck. They are then cut into small strips or "bible leaves." They look like my books. This is dangerous work. If the men fall into the water, the sharks will attack them.

▲ The crew hauls a whale aboard ship.

▲ Parts of the whale were used to make candles, perfume, umbrellas, and hoops for women's dresses.

The blubber is then boiled in big iron pots until it melts and turns into oil. The oil is cooled and put into barrels. The barrels are stored below. This whale's oil will fill about 500 barrels. We still have over 1,500 barrels to fill.

The head of the sperm whale is valuable. We separate it into three parts. From the top of the head we scoop out the purest oil, called spermaceti. Spermaceti is used for candles and hand cream. Places like Candleworks, where Granddad works, use it.

We take more oil from the whale's lower forehead. It is not as fine as spermaceti, but it is still valuable. The jaw and teeth we save for carving scrimshaw. Pedro says he will teach me to carve. I want to make a carving for Granddad.

When all the blubber has been taken from the whale, the crew looks for ambergris. It comes from the whale's intestine. It is used to make perfume, and it is worth $100 a pound! No wonder perfume costs so much.

Finally we have to clean up the ship. The ship is covered with blood. The decks are slippery. We have to carefully wash down the ship. Sharks are still out there.

CHAPTER 4

THINKING
of
HOME

We have been on this ship for well over a year. We have crossed the Atlantic Ocean many times. The lookout spots a large whaler, the *Bedford Lady*. It has come from New Bedford. Our captain decides to visit the ship. I miss home. Maybe the ship has letters for me.

The crew is excited. My friend, Pedro, tells me that the ship is a "lady's ship." It is called a lady's ship because its captain has his wife and children onboard.

Since it is almost Thanksgiving, the captains decide to celebrate together. We will share special food with the other ship.

Cook screams more. I peel lots of potatoes and vegetables and help make mince pies. The cook on the *Lady* will prepare geese and ducks. Our crew has not had meat since July 4th when we docked in Rio de Janeiro, Brazil.

We sing songs to make the work go faster. Finally, we row to the *Bedford Lady*. We board. The captains greet each other. Their captain gives us letters from home! I tear open my letter from Dad. Cook yells at me to help.

I serve the captains and officers in the stateroom. Their dinner makes my mouth water. But I want to read my letters. I read Dad's letter before I eat. It is better than food.

The Wamsutta Mills, New Bedford ▼

Dad says that I won't recognize New Bedford. The town has grown. We have a newspaper now! And there are mills that make shirts. My brother works in a cotton mill now. Men are coming to town to work in the mills, not just on whaling ships. Even the streets have changed. My sister works at the new bank. People are talking about building a free library.

New Bedford sounds like a real city. I wonder what working in a mill is like. The work can't be harder than whaling.

Thinking about New Bedford, I eat chicken with fresh vegetables and fruit. For a treat, Captain Hill gives us mince pies. I open my letter from Ma as I gobble a piece of pie.

Ma is in charge of the Spouter Inn. Her cooking is fancy now. She uses the spices that the merchant ships bring in from China and India. The ships also bring in tea and silk. Ma is saving to buy some silk.

New Bedford is rich. Some new mansions have been built on the hill. Many of the women from the top of the hill now drink tea in the afternoon like in England. Ma sells them cream and spice cakes for their tea.

My older sister has been going to meetings about ending slavery. She heard a great speaker, Frederick Douglass. She wants to help end slavery. She works in the custom house. There are many ships coming and going from New Bedford. Each ship needs papers. She works hard getting the sea captains all the papers they need.

My oldest brother now works at the Sundial Building. He makes clocks. He says that all ships at sea run on New Bedford time. Poor Granddad is working hard, too. He has little time to spend at the supply store with his friends. It seems that everyone wants candles from New Bedford. Besides, the supply store now uses the porch to sell things.

It is late at night. I have read my last letter. I look at the stars. Pedro has been teaching me how to use the stars to tell where we are. I am teaching him to write. I want to go home before New Bedford changes too much.

▲ The lighthouse guides ships into port.

GOING
HOME

Our barrels are full. Everyone will make money. The owners will keep most of the money. Captain Hill will get the most money after the owners. The officers will get less and the crew still less. I will get the least. But we have been successful. We are a "greasy" ship! We have lots of oil.

We sail home along the coast of Africa. We cross the **equator**. The days pass. Finally we stop at a port in the Azores. It is called St. Michael's. I buy a beautiful cloth for Ma. I wonder if this is what the mills make at home. I can't wait to get there.

A harbor in
▼ the Azores

▲ Barrels of whale oil on the docks at New Bedford

Pedro spots the first seagull. We are near land. Home at last! Captain Hill calls a meeting. He tells us we did well. We clean the ship for the last time. I keep looking for New Bedford. Finally we see the docks. I search for my family. I see my dad. Tears come to my eyes.

I walk home with my family. The streets are wider. There are three new stores by the docks. The Spouter Inn is larger than before. The new bank has columns like a fancy building. The streets are full of people I don't know. They are there to work in the mills or for whaling. There are many ships at the dock. Some are leaving. But I will not be sailing on them. I am home to stay. I have had my adventure. I hand Ma my gift. The cloth glistens in the sun.

Workers weave colorful patterns
▼ on cloth in this cotton mill.

EPILOGUE:
The END of WHALING

Whaling in New Bedford reached its peak in 1857. In that year, 329 ships set sail with over 10,000 men working on them. The value of the cargo and ships was more than $12,000,000.

The whaling industry slowed down. Whales became scarce. The trips became longer. One ship, *The Nile*, left in 1858 and did not return until 1869. It was gone 11 years! Other ships were lost in the frozen Arctic.

In 1859 **petroleum** was discovered in Pennsylvania. Soon petroleum was replacing whale oil in lamps and other products. People lost interest in whaling. The last whaler sailed in the 1920s.

In New Bedford, a new industry grew. Making cloth, or **textiles**, replaced whaling. Mills and machines replaced whalers. Soon everyone was working in the textile business.

Michael Shea found work in the textile mills. A hard worker, he later owned a mill. His friend Pedro worked for him. Michael moved to the top of the hill. He liked to say, "New Bedford is the best textile town in the United States!"

GLOSSARY

blacksmith – someone who makes and fits horseshoes and mends things made of iron

blubber – the fat under the skin of a whale

coast – the land along the sea

compass – an instrument for finding directions, with a magnetic needle that always points north

contract – a legal agreement in which people promise to do certain things

dock – a place where ships load and unload cargo

equator – an imaginary line around the middle of the Earth, halfway between the North and South Poles

harbor – a sheltered place along a coast where ships and boats anchor

mast – a tall pole that stands on the deck of a ship and supports its sails

petroleum – a thick, oily liquid formed underground used to make gasoline, heating oil, and many other products

port – a place where boats and ships can dock or anchor safely

scrimshaw – whalebone with carvings and design

spyglass – a small telescope

textiles – fabric or cloth that has been woven or knitted